_____

to

_____

from

_____

date

Let Me Count the Ways

Stories of the Most
Wonderful Adventure
of the Human Heart

HOWARD
PUBLISHING CO.

JIM McGUIGGAN

Our purpose at Howard Publishing is to:

- *Increase faith* in the hearts of growing Christians
- *Inspire holiness* in the lives of believers
- *Instill hope* in the hearts of struggling people everywhere

Because He's coming again!

Let Me Count the Ways © 2001 by Jim McGuiggan
All rights reserved. Printed in the United States of America

Published by Howard Publishing Co., Inc.,
3117 North 7th Street, West Monroe, LA 71291-2227

01 02 03 04 05 06 07 08 09 10   10 9 8 7 6 5 4 3 2 1

Edited by Philis Boultinghouse
Interior design by LinDee Loveland

Library of Congress Cataloging-in-Publication Data

McGuiggan, Jim, 1937-
     Let me count the ways : stories of the most wonderful adventure of the human heart /
Jim McGuiggan.
          p. cm.
     Includes bibliographical refrences (p.).
     ISBN 1-58229-156-X
          1. Love—Religious aspects—Christianity. I. Title.

BV4639 .M38 2001
242—dc21

                                                              00-050563

Scripture quotations not otherwise marked are from The Holy Bible, Authorized King James Version, © 1961 by The National Publishing Co. Other Scripture quoted from The New Testament in Modern English: Translated by J. B. Phillips (PHILLIPS), © 1958 by J. B. Phillips.

to *my Ethel*

from *her Jim*

Contents

Contents

Contents

ix

SONNET 43

How do I love thee? Let me count the ways.
I love thee to the depth and breadth and height
My soul can reach, when feeling out of sight
For the ends of Being and ideal Grace.

I love thee to the level of every day's
Most quiet need, by sun and candle-light.
I love thee freely, as men strive for Right;
I love thee purely, as they turn from Praise.

I love thee with the passion put to use
In my old griefs, and with my childhood's faith.
I love thee with a love I seemed to lose
With my lost saints—I love thee with the breath,
Smiles, tears, of all my life!—and, if God choose,
I shall but love thee better after death.

ELIZABETH BARRETT BROWNING

And when one of us is gone,
And one alone is left to carry on,
Well then, remembering will have to do,
Our memories alone will get us through,
Thinking of the days of me and you—
You and me against the world.

PAUL WILLIAMS

ONE

i love you

for making this life
a trip to remember

Don't Take the Girl

In a world where relationships can be mere surface, where commitment is often nonexistent, where the media offer rootless, sensual liaisons as the way of life—in a world like that, isn't it a genuine thrill to watch love blossom and lives become so entwined that there's no real life for either of them without the other?

I refuse to believe the media only reflect what society wants; I think they help shape those wants, and I think they exploit the weaknesses and imbalances of vulnerable people. But I also think there are hungers of a richer, deeper, finer kind out there that need to be expressed and nurtured. Couples by the countless thousands *do* shrug at the media nonsense and enjoy pleasure-filled, loving commitments. My conviction—no matter what's chic in some circles —my conviction is that people, on the whole, long for more than "help me make it through the night."

One of the most poignant love songs in recent years was written by Craig Martin and Larry Johnson and recorded by Tim McGraw. Johnny is an eight-year-old who's about to go fishing with his dad when a little girl turns up, fishing pole in hand. The boy pleads with his dad to take Jimmy Johnson or any boy in the world, but, "Please," he says, "don't take the girl."

Ten years later, the same old boy and same sweet girl, very much in love, are outside a movie theater when a stranger with a gun threatens to abduct her.

Johnny offers the gunman everything he has—money, credit cards, his grandpa's watch, car—anything, but he begs, "Please, don't take the girl."

Five years later, same lovely young couple, a baby on the way, and the mother is fading fast. He goes to his knees, fervently praying:

> Take the very breath you gave me,
> Take the heart from my chest,
> I'll gladly take her place if you want me,
> Make this my last request;
> Take me out of this world,
> God, please, don't take the girl.

With maybe less drama than depicted here, haven't we all seen or felt that very thing? Initial indifference perhaps, then tolerance, glances, smiles, moments alone, the growing pleasure, the disappointment when the other can't be there. Then the warmth, the hunger to please, the desire to touch, the early trembling kisses, and finally, the longing for more—for life together, for shared love and family.

They want someone they can dream about the future with when the sensual aspect of the relationship isn't clamoring for as much attention.

In some circles, this picture generates embarrassed grins or scornful talk of "over the top romanticism," but it's what people by the millions have experienced generation after generation; it's what men, women, girls, and boys experience and want to experience. They want passion without apology, but they want passion with someone they like, someone they enjoy spending time with, someone they can dream about the future with when the sensual aspect of the relationship isn't clamoring for as much attention. They want *life* and want it with someone who loves and admires them, someone who sees in them more than a piece of equipment that's needed to get a specific kind of buzz. Yes, it's *more* they want, not less.

But in our saner moments, I think we all understand that people don't really "fall in love"—they grow into it. And I'm guessing that that's what most people look for. They don't see "love" as one-night stands, hopping from one bed to another, seeing how many "lovers'" names they can rack up. They want the intimate, tough, and tender adventure of life with someone to whom they can whisper Browning's, "Grow old along with me! The best is yet to be." And when life is over for one of them, the other can rejoice in all that's gone before and, with a grateful, happy heart, take as their own the poet's contented words:

> When I review; my life with you
> Since the days of old,
> I wouldn't want to change it

For all the world and its gold;
If I had my life to live over,
I'd do the same things again;
I'd still want to roam
Near the place we called home,
Where my happiness never would end.
I'd meet you when school days are over,
And we'd walk down the lanes we once knew,
If I had my life to live over,
I'd still fall in love with you.

To finish the race, to have seen it through, to have bitten it off and chewed it up—that's something to be pleased about. To have done it in the company of one, just one, in glorious style, through laughter and tears, until you both lay down your tired bodies and get on out of here—that beats all to pieces the flip-flopping "till death us do part or someone better looking comes along" lifestyle a lot in Western society are offering. One girl, one boy, having a whale of a time seeing it through together! Now *that's* living!

i love you
for making
this life a trip
to remember

Take the very *breath* you gave me,

Take the *heart* from my chest,

I'll gladly take her place if you want me,

Make this my *last request;*

Take me out of this world,

God, please, don't take the girl.

Craig Martin
Larry Johnson

Such as I am, though for myself alone,
I would not be ambitious in my wish,
To wish myself much better; yet, for you
I would be trebled twenty times myself;
A thousand times more fair.

PORTIA IN
THE MERCHANT OF VENICE

TWO

i love you

*for being the strong and
sweet inspiration of my life*

9

I know there are a lot of things *called* love that don't merit the name, and I know that romance isn't the only thing that matters, but it's only hard-boiled people with too much starch in their religion who deny the power for good that romantic love brings to us all.

Have you never sat across the table from someone who so filled your heart and mind that you felt you could tackle any problem or put up with any loss? Have you never enjoyed the sheer pleasure and pain of being alone with someone who fills up your senses? Never felt what poets and lovers from Eden until now have felt—that if he or she were yours, you'd be glad to let the rest of the world go by? Haven't you, at one time or another, looked at your loved one and thought to yourself:

> I could show the world how to smile,
> I could be glad all of the while,
> I could change the gray skies to blue,
> If I had you.

In Dickens's *Great Expectations*, Pip had loved the heartless Estella since they were both children, despite the fact that she always warned him against doing it. She'd confessed she was without feeling for anyone, including Pip, so he knew what he was up against. Just the same, on one occasion when they were together in a run-down inn, his love for Estella filled his heart despite the dingy surroundings. They were sitting at a table in a large room with a fireless grate, a covering of coal dust, and a strong odor of the stable and stale soup that smelled like boiled-down horses. Even there Pip insisted, "Yet the room was all in all to me, Estella being in it." Haven't most of us been lucky enough to experience that?

After an unhappy session with Estella, with a miserable headache as well as a heartache, he made his way home and happened to meet young Jane Pocket, sister of his best friend, Herbert. She was with her young man, radiant and filled with his presence, and Pip envied him, though he knew the young man had a tough life. The youngster had Jane, and Pip was without Estella. And without her, there was a deep tear in the fabric of his life. Haven't many of us experienced that? Okay, it's true, not to have the one you love isn't the end of the world, but it's a much tougher world to live in.

Perhaps you've listened to someone rehearsing

The rejection only made him think more of her because she wouldn't cheapen herself.

the change in his life, pleased with himself. And you, without envy, reflect on the one who stood and stands by him, helping him overcome the obstacles. Your own poor little heart is beaten up. If only you had in your life the one you care deeply for, you'd make a better effort at hurdling the obstacles and rejoicing in life. You'd know what the poet meant when he sang:

> I could leave the old days behind,
> Leave all my pals,
> I'd never mind,
> I could start my life all anew,
> If I had you.

Isn't that how Dante felt about his Beatrice? The vision of her, when he was nine, stayed with him all his life and drove him to write *The Divine Comedy* and other literature and to keep his life on track. And didn't the Australian poet C. J. Dennis tell us the same thing about Bill?

Bill ran with a bad crowd to the wrong places for the wrong reasons to do the wrong things. He was on the road to nowhere, spiraling down and caring nothing about it…until he got a glimpse of Doreen. His heart was lost to her, but when he made his move in her direction, she dismissed him with a shake of the head and a lighthearted refusal. The rejection only made him think more of her because she wouldn't cheapen herself.

Ain't Love Grand

Old habits die hard, but the besotted Bill had to choose between the old ways and the girl who filled his days and nights, his dreams and his waking moments. And so…

> For 'er sweet sake I've gone and chucked it clean;
> The pubs and schools, an' all that leery game.
> For when a bloke 'as come to know Doreen,
> It ain't the same.
> There's higher things, she sez, for blokes to do;
> An' I am half believin' that it's true.

So they step out together, with Bill a changed and changing man. He has no culture, but she makes him sensitive; he isn't keen on theater or such things, but they go together to see a Shakespeare play, *Romeo and Juliet*. He'd have gone anywhere just as long as Doreen was there. Dennis has Bill tell us something about the play.

> "Lady, by yonder moon I swear!" sez 'e.
> An' then 'e climbs up on the balkiney;
> An' there they smooge a treat, wiv pretty words
> Like two love-birds.
> I nudge Doreen. She whispers, "Ain't it grand!"
> 'Er eyes is shinin'; an' I squeeze 'er 'and.

Head over heels, the world a lovelier place for both of them, problems now in perspective, someone to lean on, and the mysterious, hard-to-fathom pleasure that's now to be found in almost everything!

Two months after their wedding, Bill meets up with some of his old cronies, slips back into his old ways, and wanders home in the early hours of the morning, drunk and ashamed to see his Doreen. She puts him to bed and a few hours later tiptoes into the room with tears in her eyes and a copious supply of beef-tea (a sort of beef-bullion, commonly given to the weak). Bill is flabbergasted.

> Beef-tea! She treats me like a hinvaleed!
> Me! that had caused her loving 'eart to bleed,
> It 'urt me worse than naggin' fer a week!
> 'Er! Who had right to turn dead sour on me,
> Fergives like that, an' feeds me wif beef-tea…
> An' then—I ain't ashamed of wot I did—
> I 'ides me face…an' blubbers like a kid.

And Bill closes out the description of his life with these words:

> An' I am rich, becos my eyes 'ave seen
> The lovelight in the eye of my Doreen;
> An' I am blest becos me feet have trod
> A land 'oos fields reflect the smile o' God.

Sittin' at ev'nin' in this sunset land.
Wiv 'er in all the world to 'old me and
A son to bear me name when I am gone…
Livin' and lovin'—so life mooches on.

I can only echo the words of Doreen as she watched *Romeo and Juliet*—
"Ain't it grand!"

*i love you
for being the
strong and
sweet inspiration
of my life*

i love you

I could show the world how to *smile,*

I could be *glad* all of the while,

I could change the gray skies to blue,

If I had *you.*

Ted Shapiro
Jimmy Campbell
Reg Connelly

Love ever gives—
Forgives—outlives—
And ever stands
With open hands.
And while it lives—
It gives.
For this is love's prerogative—
To give, and give, and give.

JOHN OXENHAM

THREE

i love how you

conceal your

generosity

A Midsummer's Knight

O. Henry tells of Gaines, "the man who said he thought New York was the finest summer resort in the country." While others moaned and melted in the heat, dived for the shade or an electric fan, and wished for the mountains, he mocked the notion of going to the woods to eat canned goods from the city, being wakened in the morning by a million flies, getting soaked to the skin catching the tiniest fish and struggling up perpendicular cliffs. No sir, he preferred to stay at home. If he wanted fish, he'd go to a cool restaurant—home comforts, that's what he chose, while the fools spent half their summer driving to and from their spartan locations with all the modern *in*conveniences.

A friend urged him to come with him for two weeks to Beaverkill, where the fish were jumping at anything that even looked like a fly. He said a mutual friend, Harding, had caught a three-pound brown trout and—but Gaines was having none of it. "Nonsense!" he'd snort and then off to his office to plunge himself into a mountain of work until late in the afternoon when, with feet up on his desk, he mused to himself: "I wonder what kind of bait Harding used."

The man who said he thought New York was the finest summer resort in the country dozed off in the stifling heat, was wakened by his mail-bringing clerk, and decided to take a quick look before he left for the day. A few lines of one of them said:

My Dear, Dear Husband:

Just received your letter ordering us to stay another month…Rita's cough is almost gone…Johnny has gone wild like a little Indian…it will be the making of both children…work so hard, and I know that your business can hardly afford to keep us here so long…best man that ever…you always pretend that you like the city in summer…trout fishing that you used to be so fond of…and all to keep us well and happy…come to you if it were not doing the babies so much good…I stood last evening on Chimney Rock in exactly the same spot…when you put the wreath of roses on my head…said you would be my true knight…have always been that to me…ever and ever.

Mary

The man who said he thought New York was the finest summer resort in the country, on his way home in the sweltering summer heat, dropped into a café

I love it when those in love sometimes "tell lies" gallantly.

and had a glass of warm beer under an electric fan. "Wonder what kind of a fly old Harding used," he murmured to himself.

I love it when those in love sometimes "tell lies" gallantly. They say things no one believes—least of all themselves. They're forever making sacrifices—some large, some little—to make life easier, finer, lovelier, for those they love. They don't do it with trumpets blowing to attract attention or too sweetly, which is another form of trumpet-blowing. They don't have that pained looked, the martyr's countenance, nor do they do it with a too obvious business-as-usual appearance. No. None of that! They're in love and they do what lovers have done in every age down the centuries—they give themselves in whatever ways their love and the situation calls for.

And it's the cheerful giving nature of love that's such a glory to watch. We see it in O. Henry's Gaines, who gallantly denies himself rest and pleasure for his family's sake. Christians will say they see it best in Jesus Christ, who, with the cross staring him straight in the face, despised the shame and gladly gave himself for those he loved. And the brilliant Oxford classical scholar Gilbert Murray caught sight of it and was deeply moved. While the First World War was on, the agnostic said:

> As for me personally, there is one thought that is always with me—the thought that other men are dying for me, better men, younger, with more hope in their lives, many of whom I have taught and

loved. The orthodox Christian will be familiar with the thought of One who loved you, dying for you. I would like to say that now I am familiar with the feeling that something innocent, something great, something that loved me, is dying and dying daily for me.

These lovers aren't trying to impress anyone, not even the ones they love. It's enough for them that the love in their heart leads them to find pleasure in what they do, whether the doing is difficult or simple. While their motivation isn't to impress, they find a deep pleasure in knowing that the beloved is pleased, and that's enough for them. They live and die content. Paul Williams, one of the most sensitive songwriters since the passing of the "good old days," gets to the heart of it with this:

> And when I wake to you,
> And I pretend that I don't know
> that you've been watching me
> All the time that I lay sleeping,
> By the loving look that lingers in your eye;
> Well, that's enough for me,
> That's all the hero I need be,
> I smile to think of you and me,
> You and I,
> And how our pleasure makes me cry.

i love
how you
conceal your
generosity

And when I *wake* to you,

And I pretend that I don't know

that you've been watching me

All the time that I lay sleeping,

By the loving look that lingers in your eye;

Well, that's enough for me,

That's all the *hero* I need be,

I smile to think of you and me,

You and I,

And how our *pleasure* makes me cry.

Paul Williams

Beware of those fancies, those daydreams, which represent things as possible which should be forever impossible. Beware of that affection which cares for your happiness more than for your honor.

F. W. ROBERTSON

FOUR

i love how you

urge me to leave the good
and seek the best

Don't Shilly-Shally

Wendell Phillips, a young Harvard Law School graduate, sacrificed social status and prospective political power to fight slavery in America. In 1837 he married Ann Terry Greene, who stood by him in his war and gave him more encouragement than he could ever have expected. She was an invalid and might easily have weakened him in his driving purpose—a purpose that was very dangerous to him personally and to his reputation—but she didn't. Every night when he was going out to speak, Ralph Sockman tells us, he would go to his wife's bedside. She would take his hand in both of hers and gently say, "Don't shilly-shally tonight, Wendell!"

C. S. Lewis rightly insisted that people may love us *in spite of* our being dirty, smelly, and boorish, but they don't love us *because* of these things. If my loved one came after me because of something offensive in my life and I were to say, "If you love me that wouldn't matter," she'd have the perfect right to say, "You're wrong! It's precisely *because* I love you that it *does* matter." Because we believe that character counts, that goodness is greatness, we can't love someone without wanting the best for them. Yes, of course, we can go after it in the wrong spirit and in the wrong way, but the aim is right! Deeper lovers say to each other, "Don't shilly-shally. Pursue what's honorable."

Is there a man, woman, girl, or boy among us, with the wit to think at all, who doesn't rejoice that they have been "made better" by the one they adore? Our lovers don't weaken us. Well, yes, sometimes they do, but not in their better moments, not when they're at their best. Their love makes demands of us. You might remember the haunting and charming song by Vance and Snyder that tells of a guy in the throes of temptation, wrestling his way out of trouble by asking himself "What will my Mary say?"

He finds himself in danger of falling and says he "must hurry away" because that question keeps haunting him: "What will my Mary say?" Even more unnerving for him is this possibility:

> What would I do if she should meet me
> And find me kissing you?
> She's always trusted me completely
> Her poor heart would break in two.

You think this is only for romantic ballads? For pity's sake, no! I *know* people like this, and so do you! Even the atheist Nietzsche—hardly a sentimentalist— insisted that we act better than we are because we don't want to disappoint those we love and who love us.

But love so often acts to keep others from being hurt that we're tempted to think it should never act

We act better than we are because we don't want to disappoint those we love and who love us.

otherwise. It always seems to be giving, and we're tempted to think it makes no demands; but that's not how Wendell's wife, Ann, saw it. Nor Elizabeth Welch. When her husband, John, was imprisoned for his religious convictions during the eightenth century, the authorities didn't want to kill such an influential man so they came to Elizabeth, pleading with her to get him to recant. She listened patiently and then lifting up the ends of her apron to shape a carrying bag, she said, "Please, your majesties, I'd just as soon catch his head here."

This isn't hard and loveless! This is a lover saying, "Sweetheart, don't shilly-shally." Some of us will go down to our graves, strugglers to the end, in pursuit of purer, more consistent goodness; but we'll go with deep thanksgiving for those who were in our lives and made us finer, stronger. We'll go knowing they gave us our share of tenderness, kisses, and romance—binding us to them in all these lovely ways—but we'll recall that they helped us to look ourselves in the eye without recoiling in *utter* disappointment.

Though there's a host of us who fight terrible inner battles, my suspicion is, that for *most* of us, the awful "wrong" in our lives is not crass wickedness of the brutal and sadistic sort. For most of us, I suspect, our great wrong is the trivial nature of our lives. We're not up to our eyes in any great cause; we're deeply passionate about nothing and prefer to drift along with the nice currents, nodding approval to this good work or that, wishing it success and finding some pleasure when we hear good news about its progress.

Don't Shilly-Shally

My suspicion is that we *almost* live, that we have occasions when we want to rouse ourselves and get in over our heads in some long-lasting war against some pervasive evil that is suffocating our fellows—but we just can't get up for it. Want to get into it if for no other reason than to banish the boredom that has crept into our bones and left us with TV reruns or one more happy hour at church. This is why it's so critical for us to have friends who are passionate and vigorous, whose very bearing calls out to us, "Don't shilly-shally—get involved in life!"

Lovers like these call us out of our sleep, out of our lazy drifting, and in the name of friendship, call us to *live* life rather than fritter it away. They help us to be able to look at ourselves without suffering *too* great a sense of disappointment. They help us to make our lives count, and we bless them for it. Mark Rutherford—Christian author and theologian—put it like this: "Blessed are those who give us back our self-respect," and Roy Croft spoke his gratitude this way:

> I love you,
> Not only for what you are,
> But for what I am
> When I am with you.
>
> I love you,
> Not only for what
> You have made of yourself,
> But for what
> You are making of me.

i love
how you
urge me to leave
the good and
seek the best

i love you

I love you,

Not only for what you are,

But for what I am

When I am *with you*.

I love *you,*

Not only for what

You have made of yourself,

But for what

You are *making of me.*

Roy Croft

I [hold] it truth, with him who sings
To one clear harp in divers tones,
That men may rise on stepping-stones
Of their dead selves to higher things.

ALFRED TENNYSON

FIVE

i love how you're

with me even when

you're not there

I was speaking at a convention in a big city some time ago—not doing a great job, either, I can tell you—and was heading back to my hotel room, about fifteen minutes' walk from the meeting place. I passed a younger woman who was sitting on a low wall; I nodded and smiled at her and heard her say something in a little-girl voice. I couldn't make it out, so I stopped and asked her what she'd said. "I'm hungry," she said in the same tiny voice. I took a long look at her shabby and thin clothes, knew she couldn't have been very warm, and felt sure she could easily have been telling the truth.

I reached for some money and gave her more than enough to get herself something to eat. She rose to take the money and then said some things that made it clear it wasn't just a meal she wanted. She thought she and I could go off somewhere together and have a really nice time, and so our little conversation took off in terms something like this.

I asked her name and she said it was "Teri," and I told her mine. "So, what are you doing out here in the cold like this?" I asked her, trying to find my bearings. "I want someone to love me," she said in that same plaintive voice. "Ah, well, you're talking to the right person," I told her, "because I know someone who really loves you." She asked me who that was, and I said it was Jesus Christ.

Her disappointment registered plainly. "But I want *you* to love me," she said, reaching for my hand; "I want to be touched. I want you to make love to me." I held on to her hand, moved closer to her, and gently told her I couldn't do that, and she wanted to know why. I told her I was married, but she said she didn't mind.

I said to her, "But, Teri, what would my Ethel say?"

She didn't know, but she told me: "You could tell her it was good."

"But it *wouldn't* be good, Teri," I told her. "Not for you, me, or anyone else." I spoke to her about the Master as I put my arm around her and moved her in the direction of a sandwich shop across the street. She asked me where I was going, and I said, "To my hotel—" When she jumped in to offer to go with me, I smiled and said with conviction, "On…my…own." I said something about maybe seeing her again; she smiled, and the last I saw of her, she was crossing the street to the eating place.

Poor girl. Maybe at another time and under other circumstances she'd have had a slim chance of success, but I was too filled—this is going to make me sound too noble, but I'll take the risk—I was too filled with

One face, one heart, one name can make us strong at the critical moment.

37

compassion for the girl, too aware of my place as Christ's servant, and too filled with a sense of Ethel to do anything other than what was right…and kind.

Experiencing a warm triumph like that helps us believe there can be a whole life of warm triumphs. Just one can keep us from despairing. Just one…clear…victory (not over a person and not with an air of smug self-righteousness)—just one can save our whole lives by keeping us from complete despair and the ultimate ruin that self-loathing so often leads to.

And seeing a lovely man or woman of faith enables us to believe there *can* be millions like them and helps us to believe that goodness is possible even for us.

Arthur Gossip, speaking of our influence via personality, for good or evil, said he'd had the privilege of working with Alexander Cumming of Forfar. A man, Gossip said, who wasn't known far beyond the local boundaries of his town—a town that wasn't given to much emotion. But the town held Cumming in reverence.

> As the tall, stooping, venerable figure moved about the streets, pausing to pet a bairn, or slipping up close on yet another of the endless little kindnesses with which he crowded his happy days, faces everywhere lit up at the sight of him; and people, their voices suddenly grown softer, became kindlier in conversation when he hove into sight. So he passed to and fro, a kind of benediction to us all, as if

God's own hand had been laid in tenderness upon us. I well remember how one of the chief men in the place, strong, self-reliant, and with many admirable qualities, but not one whom you would have thought could be easily touched, looked after him one day. "Often I pull myself together with this thought," he said, "that if I threw away my life, I think I could bear my punishment without whining, but...but"—and the man's voice sagged a little—"I could not face the pain in Mr. Cumming's eyes."

One face, one heart, one name can make us strong at the critical moment, despite powerful temptations that are strengthened by inner shaping and outward circumstances. And with a heart thankful to God for that one face, that one name, we can bring the lovely triumph out from time to time and gain perspective and purpose and further strength from it.

People like you and me, for all our shortcomings, want to be straight people in a bent world, want to be compassionate in a hard world. Not only do I truly not want to do anything that would shame Ethel, I don't even want to do anything that would embarrass her if she got to hear of it. What Ethel would think about my behavior may not always redeem me from failure, but how could it *not* be an influence that protects me and anyone I might injure?

I hope there's someone in your life who loves you so much that the very thought of him or her gives you strength to be gallant in your pursuit of truth and a lovely life.

i love how you're
with me
even when
you're not there

i love you

Experiencing a warm triumph

helps us *believe*

there can be a whole life

of *warm triumphs.*

Just one can keep us from despairing.

"Good-bye," said the fox. "And now here is my secret, a very simple secret: It is only with the heart that one can see rightly; what is essential is invisible to the eye."

ANTOINE DE SAINT-EXUPÉRY

i love you

for seeing in me
more than i can

If you remember Mr. Wilkins Micawber and his wife, Emma, from the Dickens novel *David Copperfield*, you'll know they were hardly the perfect models for living. Wilkins Micawber himself admitted that he was unwise with money, that he was a dreamer even when *doing* was more to the point, that he was a procrastinator and something of a genteel parasite who gave out good advice without taking it himself. Mrs. Micawber had her own failings, which included a constant harping back to the better days she had before marriage to Mr. Micawber (as she insisted on calling him).

Micawber was forever in trouble over money (more precisely, the lack of it) and spent time dodging his creditors or facing judges or settling himself in at the debtors prison. Despite the hardships Mrs. Micawber and her four children had to endure as a result of all this, she insisted with passion: "I will never desert Mr. Micawber!" Indeed, once when she was giving forth to David Copperfield, she astounded the boy by saying to him, "But I will never desert Mr. Micawber. No! I never will do it! It's of no use asking me!" The shocked David wanted to assure her he never had nor would he ever ask her to do anything of the sort, but she continued to proclaim her loyalty with a passion that simply silenced and frightened him.

Having said all that, the pair knew how to enjoy the pleasures of life as surely as they knew how to lament the miseries that they helped generate. They "sinned bravely" (as Luther would put it). In his "airhead" way,

Wilkins was always "expecting something to turn up," and Mrs. Micawber believed her husband's great talent would see them through—if only those above him would give him the chance to shine and if Micawber himself would do a little more to *help* things "turn up."

And it's *that* about Emma Micawber—however skewed her way of seeing it was—that makes her one of my favorite characters. Her husband's endless blunders, his obvious weaknesses, and his litany of failures couldn't hide from her "the great talent" and power she saw in Mr. Micawber. True, her necklaces and bracelets, silver spoons, and finally their furniture were sold out from under them—all this she acknowledged (sometimes with too much of the martyr spirit), but she loved him and made him believe he could make things right, indeed, *would* make them right. Her family saw Mr. Micawber as of no account, but "the loss" she observed, "has been my family's, not yours."

When Micawber exposes the infamous Uriah

She believed he had it in him to have it in him.

Heep and saves families from financial ruin, the grateful parties give the Micawbers all they need to emigrate. Wilkins says he is cutting his ties with England, but his wife insists, "You do not know your own power, Micawber…shall I be so weak as to imagine that Mr. Micawber, wielding the rod of talent and of power in Australia, will be nothing in England?…Mr. Micawber may be—I cannot disguise from myself that the probability is, Mr. Micawber will be—a page of history."

The dithering husband hears her words and can't help but be strengthened by her confidence. He says, "My love, it is impossible for me not to be touched by your affection. I am always willing to defer to your good sense."

And so it goes on. She believes in him and expects great things from him. She confesses not only her love for him but her *need* of him; and though she knows full well that his character is flawed, she believes he will finally triumph. According to her, Micawber *thinks* he knows his power and potential, but she's sure he doesn't, and she wants him to stand on the prow of the ship that carries him to the new continent and shout, "This country I am come to conquer! Have you honors? Have you riches? Have you posts of profitable pecuniary emolument? Let them be brought forward. They are mine."

This she says of a man she knows to be flawed, calling him to greater heights than he has known, greater heights than she *knows* he has known. And this is part of what makes me an ardent admirer of Mrs. Micawber.

Can you remember what A. J. Gordon told his readers about the two groups of struggling writers he was acquainted with, who gathered regularly to read their work to each other? The men's group was called "the Stranglers," and the women's was called "the Wranglers." The Stranglers crucified one another's work with savage criticisms, pointing out too plainly the obvious failings in the efforts, while the Wranglers kept looking until they could say something positive about everyone's work. Out of the group of men, not one made it as a noted writer; but out of the women there were several, including the author of *The Yearling*.

To realize we're loved and that there's nothing we can do to change that is critically important, but if that essential truth is made the only truth, it can injure us. It can place us in the role of permanent "takers" when we need to be "givers." We need to be givers for our own soul's sake, so we can be full human beings, so we won't become like lap dogs, always being pampered and petted by someone whose love asks nothing of us. Ugh!

For all her naiveté, Emma Micawber expected something of her air-headed husband, made demands of him because she believed he had it in him to have it in him. If he didn't have it now, he *could* and *would* have it. Her love of him didn't blind her to his flaws. Her need of him and belief in him is part of what kept him from doing further damage when he (unconvincingly) raised a razor in the direction of his throat—bringing a cry of fear to Emma's lips.

I'm sure you remember "You Needed Me," a song made popular by Canadian singer Anne Murray. A piece of it says:

> I cried a tear; you wiped it dry,
> I was confused; you cleared my mind,
> I sold my soul; you bought it back for me,
> And held me up, and gave me dignity,
> Somehow you needed me.

And that phrase recurs throughout the song—"You needed me!" The song's filled with lovely things the lover does, but a central part of it all is this: The loved one felt *needed*, felt there was something she could give, felt she was useful. Now there's a redeeming factor: the belief that we have something to contribute, the conviction that we're not just "pretty faces."

For all the humor in Dickens's creation and for all its fiction, there's a joyful seriousness and bedrock truth in the sketches. And I think of my own "Mrs. Micawber," who down the years—when observers saw me (with good reason) as seriously flawed—insisted and insists to this day that it's in me (by

God's grace) to have it in me to win in the end and to do some people some good on the way.

So here's to all the "Mrs. Micawbers" in the world who keep their painfully comic, airheaded, moon-gazing, bumbling Micawbers from ending their days in a debtors prison.

i love you
for seeing in me
more than
i can

i love you

I *cried* a tear; you wiped it dry,

I was confused; you *cleared* my mind,

I *sold my soul;* you bought it back for me,

And held me up, and gave me dignity,

Somehow *you needed me.*

Anne Murray

And maddest of all; to see life as it is and not as it could be, as it should be.

DALE WASSERMAN

i love how you

nod to appearance but
go to the heart of things

When Dr. Allain entered a hospital room to work on Alvin Richardson, whose feet were dying, the heavy odor in the room told him he'd be engrossed in his work for a while. As he unwrapped the soggy bandage on one foot that had a large, draining wound, he tried to get Alvin to talk. But the poor man was lost in a fog of illness and medicine, so the doctor worked in silence. He didn't hear the first *pop* or the second and third, but they began to work their way into his consciousness by the time he heard the fourth and fifth. They were spaced irregularly, as much as two or three minutes apart, some softer than others. With the sixth one, he turned to trace the sound and discovered someone else was in the room.

"I'm sorry," he said to the person on the other side of the room, sitting in a low wheelchair with his back to him, "I didn't see you. You startled me."

There was no response, and he approached the man.

"Have you been there all the time?"

In front of the wheelchair was an ancient typewriter, and as Allain watched, an arm flung itself from the man's body, bending and winding as though it had more joints than it should. Then the other arm shot up to join its partner, both of them struggling in the air, while the man's huge head tipped forward on his neck and then turned to look up at the right hand, squinting to get it in his sights. With a sudden, violent jerk, the hand was brought down on the typewriter, and *pop*, the index finger struck a key. The man was typing!

His trousers, suspended at the shoulders, were more than roomy. His shoes, black and heavy, were old but unmarked—he did no walking. From out of a gray undershirt, white arms and neck protruded, but his lips were surprisingly red and were pulled into a grimace that might even have been a smile.

Allain said hello and a voice, no more controlled than the arms, replied, "A-ow."

"What's your name?"

"A-Arold."

"Harold?"

"Ayss."

"Have you been here long?"

"Ayss."

"What are you writing?"

"A ledder."

"How long does it take you to write a letter?"

"A mon."

"A month?"

"Ayss."

The doctor saw that the page was three quarters covered and moved close enough to see with a quick glance that it began with "My dearest Vera."

Love isn't just for the "beautiful people." It's for anyone with a heart.

This man was writing to a woman and calling her "my" and "dearest"! Allain couldn't help himself and moved a little closer to scan the page. Words ran together, letters were crossed out with Xs (after so much effort, he often hit the wrong key!), and lines were sometimes slanted wildly. But it was a warm and beautiful love letter.

When Allain looked down, Harold was grinning up at him. There was no accusation or resentment about his letter being read, but there was no apology either that a man in a body like his would be writing such a letter. The doctor glanced at Harold's night table, and there amid the clutter of tissues, loose crackers, and postcards, he saw a picture of a beautiful woman and a note written on it, signed with a flourish: "To Harold with love" and underneath that, the name Joan Crawford.

The surgeon nodded slightly toward the photograph.

"Vera?" he asked quietly.

"Ayss," Harold grinned.

Who'd have thought it? Who'd have thought a man as outwardly unpromising as Harold would dream such lovely dreams? But he's our judge, isn't he? *Judge Harold!*

There he is, wrapped in a body not quite under his control, isolated behind closed doors in a hospital room and surrounded by the fragrance of death! And what's he doing? He's thinking of "Vera" and how he loves her.

He's dreaming his dreams and giving his lovely longings to her in a way that's quite beyond so many of the heartless and dreamless *takers*.

Love isn't just for the "beautiful people," with their stunning good looks and oceans of charisma. It's for anyone with a heart. It's for people who can take their eyes off themselves long enough to be warmed and moved by the mystery and glory of another soul. Love is for everyone who can dream. Love is for those who, instead of a ceaseless, "Here I am! Here I am!" can say with breathless pleasure, "Ah, there you are." Yes, it's a matter of heart rather than intellect, a question of soul rather than body; it's about inner reality rather than appearance.

In the 1956 movie *Forever Darling*, a guardian angel comes to help a marriage that is slowly crumbling. The zest was going out of it, and the pair were drifting apart because their relationship was grounded more in appearance and externals than in the deeper structures. In one scene, the angel says to the sad wife, who hasn't been able to come to terms with the changes the years had brought:

> Let me tell you a story. I once knew a man with the face of a mountain goat. His wife loved him very, very much. She thought he was utterly charming, but the truth was he dribbled when he ate and he was cross-eyed and bald and fat. He had all sorts of human habits that would have irritated her very much if she hadn't been in love.

And do you know why she loved him? The man with the face of a mountain goat had the heart of an Abraham Lincoln, and she was wise enough to know this. So, to her, he was always...something more than a man, there was something of God in him. And he never stopped loving her because he knew that she understood what he was, and he loved her for it! And he never noticed the wrinkles coming or the hair growing grey. Their love was deep, so it lasted. They had a *wonderful* life.

Lovers don't deny that physical beauty exists. It's just that they don't and won't *worship* it. We see the truth of this every time we see a really pretty girl in love with an unattractive man or a handsome man with a plain-looking girl. We see it when parents unashamedly adore deformed children and when friends—young and old—long for each other's company irrespective of appearances. The lovers not only *see* something more important than external good looks, they are *drawn* by what they see. In the most unpromising places, faces, and figures, those who are willing to give as well as take have found the ecstasy of both giving and receiving.

Doesn't it just warm your heart to find such a tender spirit in a body like Harold's? Doesn't it just smash to smithereens our smug, know-it-all tendencies? How dare we presume to know from externals what is going on inside! What fools we are to make visible accomplishment or appearance the only criterion of worthiness. Proud Pharisees need to think carefully, for the One who comes to dinner in their houses won't see as they see or think as they think. His eyes may rest approvingly on someone they have labeled and rejected.

And the letter written by Harold? What did it say? Read this and smile and let love open your eyes to its presence in the most unexpected places.

> My dearest Vera,
>
> There is such a bustle and stir at the hotel. It is as though we will be visited today by an important personage. A queen or an archangel or, wild wild hope, by you, my darling. Nothing else would explain the "high" one senses here today. A dozen times I have turned from my book to peer expectantly down the road. Even the lilies at the gate are bobbing and ducking to get a better view....
>
> Well, we shall try to keep from going mad with anticipation. Perhaps a walk will help. My neighbor here, old Richardson, is an indefatigable walker. Not heath nor steppe, not veldt nor mesa, is safe from his clodhoppers. I myself am an ambler, a meanderer. I don't like to butt into Nature's business. She knew what she was about, arranging her grass and the sand that way. It doesn't need my boot to sock it askew. No, ma'am. I slither through the blades like a little green snake, leaving it all arranged just as Nature put it.
>
> Oh, Vera, hurry back to me. Man cannot live forever by whimsy and caprice. And I must get back to the serious work of my life— you, my magnum opus, my unicorn. Your last letter should have been written in light on hummingbird's wings. It is love o'erfused with air. To be loved by you is all in all....

i love how
you nod to
appearance but
go to the heart
of things

i love you

Oh, Vera, hurry back to me. Man cannot live *forever* by whimsy and caprice. And I must get back to the serious work of my life— you, my *magnum opus*, my unicorn. Your last letter should have been written in light on hummingbird's wings. It is *love* o'erfused with air. *To be* loved by you is all in *all*...

Harold

Without love, who'd want to live forever?… What makes eternal life a desirable thing is life, not eternity.

EIGHT

i love you

for helping me
want to live forever

Ethel, Loss, and Ethel Again

Not long ago my wife, Ethel, underwent another major surgery. In the course of performing a urostomy, the surgeon found her intestinal tract to be one mass of tissue, stuck together and stuck to the wall of the peritoneal cavity. During the process, the colon suffered a tear, and because of her complex medical condition (among other things), the surgeon performed a temporary (transverse) colostomy and wheeled her into the recovery room. A little later I was allowed in. I can still see it vividly.

Everywhere there are tubes, leads, pads, oxygen masks, antibiotic drips, fluid lines, BP armlets, nasogastric lines, catheters, hypodermics, monitors, wound drains, beeps, clicks, thuds, wheezes, morphine dispensers, curtains, swabs, disciplined nurses and doctors giving and taking instructions—and in the middle of all this, my Ethel. Flushed, deep red, badly swollen, deep panting one moment, shallow breathing the next, gagging, turning her head from one side to the other, eyes rolling, opening and shutting, lips moving under the oxygen mask as she tries to tell somebody—anybody—tries to tell them something. Her eyes open, startled and anxious, and dart around the room. She sees me beside her bed, fractionally loses the panic, rolls her eyes at me, and goes back to gagging, while the hot, swollen fingers I'm holding tremble and twitch.

I'd thought for a long time that I wanted to die before Ethel, but I've changed my mind. Her panicky search for me in the middle of her chaos, the assurance that registered in that split second changed my mind. If she went first, I'd miss her terribly—my friend above all other friends in life—but I'd hate her to die, as die she will one day, looking around in panic for the one face she wants to see above any other.

It isn't that I'm such a wonderful husband and friend; it's that she sees me that way. Joseph Stowell, president of Moody Bible Institute in Chicago, said that if God were in the "commuting language" habit, as so many motorists are, he would hang a little yellow card around the neck of sinners that reads "Precious to God!" Well said! If Ethel were in the commuting language habit, she'd hang a yellow card around my neck, reading "Precious to Ethel!"

I'm just another one of the many millions who can't easily bear watching their loved ones going through frequent episodes of acute trauma on top of chronic illness, but each one of us has to suffer for his or her own.

It isn't that I'm such a wonderful husband and friend; it's that she sees me that way.

In feeling my pain over Ethel, I can better understand your pain over your loved ones, even though I don't know you personally. And as you read this, you'll be able to sense my pain because you have a deep love for someone who's enduring a physical purgatory. And so we learn to join hearts with strangers in this global fellowship of suffering.

All this anxiety and pain is part of the price we pay for loving one another, isn't it? It's a price we aren't always keen to pay, but when the bill comes due, we gladly pay it. We'd rather be humans deeply committed in love to one another than contented cabbages. We don't want to be *less* than human, so we're more than willing to take whatever being fully human and fully alive brings.

You might remember Aldous Huxley's *Brave New World*. It's a world where life is completely mapped out for us by those in power who take all the pain and inconvenience out of life. With their genetic engineering, drugs, and conditioning, life's troubles are banished. One of the rebels against the system is protesting to the Controller, Mustapha Mond, about the suffocation of life that's resulted from all the "progress." Mond says, "We prefer to do things comfortably," and the Savage flames back: "But I don't want comfort. I want God, I want poetry, I want real danger, I want freedom, I want goodness, I want sin."

The Controller says, "In fact, you're claiming the right to be unhappy," and the Savage defiantly tells him, "All right, then, I'm claiming the right to be unhappy." Mond reminds him of the things that could come his way, like disease, anxiety, and unspeakable pain. A long silence follows as the Savage reflects on it before he says, "I claim them all." And so do we; we claim them all.

I'm compelled to say that I've never been more pleased that Ethel and I are friends in Christ, because that means, as I reminded her one day, we're friends forever! And if heaven is a place where—in God's gladdening presence—old and dear friends hold each other again, life here is finer and the future lovelier. And saying that reminds me of one of Robert Browning's poems, "Prospice."

He wrote it shortly after the death of his wife, Elizabeth Barrett Browning (formerly one of the Barretts of Wimpole Street). He adored the woman, and she felt the same way about him, so her death was all the more a test of his character and philosophy. What will he now say of death and life, now that the walls have tumbled in on him? Will he still be that vibrant lover of life who said he wanted to taste it all, who wanted to live life to the full and so "earn death"? He was fully assured that God would do what was right, and with that settled, he set his mind on seeing his Elizabeth again.

Fear death?—to feel the fog in my throat,
	The mist in my face,
When the snows begin, and the blasts denote
	I am nearing the place,
I was ever a fighter, so—one fight more,
	The best and the last!
I would hate that death bandaged my eyes, and forebore,
	And bade me creep past.
No! let me taste the whole of it, fare like my peers
	The heroes of old,
Bear the brunt, in a minute pay glad life's arrears
	Of pain, darkness and cold.
For sudden the worst turns the best to the brave,
	The black minute's at end,
And the elements' rage, the fiend-voices rave,
	Shall dwindle, shall blend,
Shall change, shall become first a peace out of pain,
	Then a light, then thy breast,
O thou soul of my soul! I shall clasp thee again,
	And with God be the rest!

Eternal life isn't mere endless existence—it's fullness of life that doesn't end. Without love, who'd want to live forever? Without friends and the joy of sweet, strong relationships, who'd want to go on endlessly? What makes eternal life a desirable thing is life, not eternity. And as long as Ethel lives, I would want to live. You who love and are loved know exactly what I mean. For you who have found God together, the sequence is: love, loss, and love again.

i love you
for helping
me want to live
forever

Fear death?—*to feel* the fog in my throat,

The mist in my face,

When the *snows* begin, and the blasts denote

I am nearing the place,

I was ever a fighter, so—*one fight more,*

The *best* and the last!

Robert Browning

So many times when the city seems
to be without a friendly face,
A lonely place;
It's nice to know that you'll be
there if I need you
And you'll always smile,
"It's all worthwhile"…

PAUL WILLIAMS

NINE

i love how you

*enter my fears
and ease them*

You and Me against the World

I read someone, somewhere, saying that nothing strengthens us like a cry for help. I believe that! I'm speaking my sincere conviction when I say that I see myself as anything but a model husband, but few things strengthen and inspire me more than when Ethel looks to me for protection or help. Nothing focuses my attention quicker than seeing her in real need or distress; nothing makes me forget my weaknesses more completely.

If she's ill in the hospital, she hates it when I pursue doctors or nurses too bluntly, when I think they're not treating her right. Once when I did that and she was distressed with me, in my irritation I told her I'd say nothing more to any of them! But a day or two later, when they were wheeling her to the theater for the very serious surgery, she took my hand and beckoned with her eyes. I leaned over her and she whispered into my ear, "Will you watch out for me?" My sulk fell dead at my feet, I reproached myself for my childishness, and at the same time, I was filled with an overwhelming tenderness toward my dearest of all friends. I don't remember precisely what I said, but I whispered my love for her, kissed her fear-filled face, and promised I'd look after her. How could I have been such a jerk?

Paul Williams and Ken Ascher wrote the poignant "You and Me against the World." A piece of it goes like this:

Remember when the circus came to town,
You were frightened by the clown,
Wasn't it nice to be around,
Someone that you knew,
Someone who was big and strong
And looking out for you—
And me against the world…

My sulk fell dead at my feet, and I reproached myself for my childishness.

When I married the girl all those years ago, I vowed, among other things, that I'd protect her; and she took me seriously. My failures in more than forty-three years of marriage would fill a fairly large volume from end to end (did I say one volume?), but some-where in the middle of all those years, maybe…just maybe, I've had an honest shot at being there when she was "frightened by the clowns."

In a world of tough, competent businesswomen who lead large corporations and national newspapers, in a world that's produced Florence Nightingales, Mother Teresas, and Margaret Thatchers, I'm not interested in claiming that women are helpless little weaklings—I know better than that. Still, I hope the day never comes when men stop feeling protective toward the women they adore. Yes, they should work at knowing the difference between suffocation and protection, but gallantry is still great!

Wasn't it gallantry the biblical Ruth banked on when she and her aged mother-in-law were in trouble? She came to an older man, Boaz, pleading for help, and he—aware of her goodness and strength but seeing her vulnerability—was drawn to her and entered her life to stay.

Here's something L. A. Banks, Christian theologian and author, came across:

> How many there are who fail in life's struggles through lack of sympathy and the inspiration which is born of it. A physician recently related an incident that came under his observation. He was counting the flagging pulse of a very sick woman who seemed to have no desire to prolong her life of semi-starvation in heart and body, when her husband, a morose, hard-visaged man, drew near the bed, and with a dry sob in his voice said, "Save her, doctor; I couldn't live without her!" The woman opened her half-closed eyes, and a slight flush crept over her withered cheek. "Did you say that, Joe? Then I'll live." And with a happy sigh, she fell into a sleep that was the beginning of recovery.

There's something in all this I can't quite put my finger on. It's very precious to me, but I can't quite grasp it. When I say what comes to my mind, it sounds right, but it doesn't get to the bottom of it, so I'm going to have to leave it unfathomed. I know this: Joe's need of this dear woman dragged her up from the grave. His pitiful confession was all she needed to inspire her and enable her to throw herself back into a terrific battle with life in the company of someone she adored. Love just can't resist a cry for help.

i love
how you enter
my fears and
ease them

i love you

Remember when the circus came to town,

You were frightened by the clown,

Wasn't it nice to be around,

Someone that you knew,

Someone who was *big and strong*

And looking out for you—

And me against the world...

Paul Williams
Ken Ascher

You only have I known of all
the families of the earth.

AMOS 3:2

i love you

for thinking "i'm a royal waste of time"

Tamed

What's so special? About your loved one, I mean—what makes him or her special? Is she the prettiest woman in the world? Is he the handsomest man? Is she the wittiest or wisest? Is he the most patient or generous or charming person on earth? Or is it something that might include some of those qualities to some degree but goes beyond them? Something that involves that kind of thing but isn't identified with them?

Isn't it true that it's our *history* with those we love that makes them special? Just the simple fact that—whatever else is true about them—they're "ours." Not ours in the sense of possession, ours in relationship. We've spent time with them, experienced so much with them, wept, laughed, hungered, slept, picnicked, anguished, read, watched, listened, ate, fought—and a thousand other things—with them!

I have no history with the gorgeous stranger. Whatever else she could be to me or I to her, she can't be "mine" or I hers. If we're to *cherish*, there's no substitute for experiencing life together.

Antoine de Saint-Exupéry's life story reads like a Robert Louis Stevenson adventure. Born into an impoverished aristocratic family in Lyons, he was a poor student who failed the entrance exam to the Naval College. A licensed pilot at twenty-two, he became an airmail pilot, flying routes over northwest Africa, the South Atlantic, and South America. He later became a test pilot and then a newspaper reporter. He had numerous airplane crashes, which left him with permanent disabilities, but in 1943 he rejoined the air force in North Africa and was shot down on a reconnaissance mission. He met death on a flight over the Mediterranean in July 1944.

Toward the end of his brief forty-four years, Saint-Exupéry's view of humans became sadder and more pessimistic. But, despite that, and in spite of his own adventure-filled life, he left behind a marvelous book called *The Little Prince*, which insists that the best things in life are still the simplest ones, and they're the ones that involve the gracious capacity to give and receive. This message also comes through loud and clear: If you have one genuine, loving relationship, it makes the world a lovelier place to live.

The little prince lived on a very tiny planet—so tiny that he could see the sun rise and set forty-four times a day. He enjoyed taking care of his planet, with its tiny volcanoes, a sheep, simple flowers, and

"It is the time you have wasted for your rose that makes your rose so important."

the baobab seeds. The baobab trees couldn't be allowed to grow because they were so large and their roots ran so deep that they would split the whole planet apart, so he was always engaged in weeding them out.

One day, from who knows where, a seed floated onto his planet—a rose seed. He'd never seen a rose before, but he watered and nourished it, and the rose became beautiful, though with its beauty came vanity, pride, and an insistence on being catered to. Despite the new and lovely fragrance and the beauty and glory of the rose, the little prince grew weary of her silly talk and her self-centeredness. For all the rose's dependence on him, she seemed to think she could do without him because she had "claws," by which she meant her thorns. Naively, she thought these were terrible weapons with which she could defeat even tigers (when the truth was, they couldn't even protect her against a sheep that would eat her and her thorns without even noticing the thorns were there).

Her speech made him unhappy, and though she confessed fault, he decided to go to other planets and seek friends. After a series of meetings with various people, it began to dawn on the little prince that people had a strange way of determining what was or wasn't important. But imagine his surprise when one day he walked by a garden on earth and found five thousand roses that looked exactly like his rose. He was filled with sadness for his rose who had told him she was the only one in all the universe. He knew that if she saw them all, she would be so shamed that she'd cough terribly and pretend she was dying and he'd have to pretend he was nursing her back to life or she really *would* let herself die. Somehow, her uniqueness must be maintained.

But then it occurred to him that he wasn't as rich as he'd thought he was. He had seen himself as having the only rose in the universe, when in reality she was only one of thousands. This made him sad as well, and he cried in disappointment.

It was then he met the fox. An untamed fox, who was under an apple tree and who couldn't play with the little prince when he asked him to because, as he said, "I am not tamed." And what did "tamed" mean, the boy who was looking for friends wanted to know.

"It means to establish ties," said the fox. "To me, you are still nothing more than a little boy who is just like a hundred thousand other little boys.... To you, I am nothing more than a fox like a hundred thousand other foxes. But if you tame me, then we shall need each other. To me, you will be unique in all the world. To you, I shall be unique in all the world."

It began to dawn on the boy that there was a flower out there in the heavens that had tamed him. So the little prince tamed the fox, they established ties, and they became friends. Not long before the boy had to leave, the fox said, "Go and look again at the roses. You will understand now that yours is unique in all the world. Then come back to say good-bye to me, and I will make you a present of a secret."

And the boy did look at them again and felt compelled to say: "You are not at all like my rose...no one has tamed you, and you have tamed no one. You are like my fox when I first knew him. He was only a fox like a hundred thousand other foxes. But I have made him my friend, and now he is unique in all the world."

And the roses were very much embarrassed. "You are beautiful, but you are empty," he went on. "One could not die for you. To be sure, an ordinary passerby would think that my rose looked just like you—the rose that belongs to me. But in herself alone she is more important than all the hundreds of you other roses: because it is she that I have watered; because it is she that I have put under the glass globe; because it is she that I have sheltered behind the screen; because it is for her that I have killed the caterpillars (except the two or three that we saved to become butterflies); because it is she that I have listened to, when she grumbled, or boasted, or even sometimes when she said nothing. Because she is *my* rose." And he went back to the fox.

"Good-bye," said the fox. "And now here is my secret, a very simple secret: It is only with the heart that one can see rightly; what is essential is invisible to the eye…. It is the time you have wasted for your rose that makes your rose so important."

Something of that occurs in the movie *Good Will Hunting*. Will is a mathematical genius whose life is a shambles, but he has the good fortune to make a friend of Sean Maguire, a psychologist whose wife died two years earlier—terribly missed. Maguire is telling the shattered young man that if relationships are to be built and last, they must accept the "imperfections" of everyone involved. He tells Will personal things about his wife, things that aren't flattering, but joyfully insists that they're the things that make for intimacy. "She's been dead two years," he said, "and that's the stuff I remember. Wonderful stuff, you know, little things like that that happen, those are the things I miss the most. Her little idiosyncrasies that only I know about. That's what made her my wife…. People call these 'imperfections,' but they're not. Ah, they're the good stuff. Then we get to choose who we will let into our weird little world…that's what makes for intimacy."

This is what Saint-Exupéry's fox was telling the little prince. Just as no two roses are the same once someone has "wasted time" with one, so no pair of lovers, no pair of friends, no husband-wife team is like any other. Love is words, but it's more than words, and marriage is more than solemn vows on a piece of paper. It's "wasting time" with each other, learning the "imperfections" of each other and shrouding them in mystery and intimacy. It's learning the real weaknesses of each other and, in loving, hiding a multitude of sins.

The little prince later confessed that he had taken the rose's *words* and her shortcomings too seriously.

> One never ought to listen to the flowers. One should simply look at them and breathe their fragrance. Mine perfumed all my planet. But I did not know how to take pleasure in all her grace. This tale of claws, which disturbed me so much, should only have filled my heart with tenderness and pity. The fact is that I did not know how to judge anything! I ought to have judged by deeds and not words. She cast her fragrance and her radiance over me. I ought never to have run away from her.... I ought to have guessed all the affection that lay behind her poor little stratagems. Flowers are so inconsistent! But I was too young to know how to love her.

Saint-Exupéry's philosophy of life wasn't rich enough, but it wasn't without riches. The story has so much to say to us about life and living. With God's blessing there's a day coming when we'll fully understand that what begins to make the whole world a lovely place is concrete, personal, loving relationships. We'll understand—and be enriched by understanding—that it's by actually *having* a friend that we are able to make sense of and appreciate the friendships of all other people; it's by the pain we feel in our losses that we are able to enter into the pain of the losses of all others. When we run to the defense of our loved ones, we'll know why others run to the defense of theirs. When we make excuses for the acknowledged wrongdoing of our friends, we'll know why others do the same. In caring for and committing to specific people, we are given the opportunity to understand and admire a world of caring and commitment by others.

So questions like, "What does she see in him?" become pointless. They've "tamed" each other; and because each is in the world, it has become a warmer, more glorious and cheerful place. Hasn't this happened to us, Christian and non-Christian alike?

The Christian would insist, of course, with G. K. Chesterton, that two thousand years ago a man came into our world, and since He's been here, we can't look at a tree, a blade of grass, a loaf of bread, a suffering human, a joy-filled heart, a loving couple or a case of injustice without thinking of Him.

All of that and more because He has "tamed" us.

i love you
for thinking
"i'm a royal
waste of time"

i love you

If you tame me, then we shall *need*

each other.

To me, you will be *unique* in all the world.

To you, I shall be unique in *all the world*.

Antoine de Saint-Exupéry

If you can make a heap of all your
winnings,
And risk them at one turn of
pitch-and-toss and lose,
And start again at your beginnings
And never breathe a word about
your loss…

RUDYARD KIPLING

i love how you

gallantly pretend

Welsh Rabbit in the Afternoon

It's a mistake to think we can live full lives without the beauty and glories of daily heroic behavior. These things shape us and keep us hopeful. They're the whisper of God that the world isn't inexorably destined to be an utter sewer; they're the voice of God saying he hasn't deserted us (praise him!).

We hear an almost constant stream of bad news and tragedies, of stunning evil and cold cruelty. It's a wonder we aren't cynics with dead souls by now. What helps us to defy the notion of evil's complete triumph is the spellbinding, glorious presence of heroism and gallantry, to be seen any day in every city, town, and village across the world. Here's a fictional account of what, in fact, is everyday behavior.

When Joe Larrabee was six years old, he drew a picture of the town pump with a prominent citizen scampering past it. That's when everyone knew he was a budding genius, and some years later they urged him in the direction of New York to study under the noted Magister, though Joe was as poor as a church mouse at the time.

Delia Caruthers was an enchantress on the piano, so there was nothing for her parents and friends to do but send her to study under Rosenstock—in New York.

That's where they met, and before they knew it, they were Mr. and Mrs. Larrabee, living in a tiny apartment, with Joe acting as janitor to make ends meet. They were optimistic, and before you know it, they told each other,

Delia would be playing to packed houses and having lobster dinners in private dining rooms and Joe would be selling paintings to upper-crust people for obscene amounts of money.

Meanwhile, they adored each other. Their pleasure at one another's presence, the excited talk about their studies and their work, sharing the new things they had learned, being thrilled by their mutual progress—all that made tiny breakfasts and cheese sandwiches at 11:00 P.M. no real hardship.

But money was going out and none was coming in, so Delia said she'd have to give up her music lessons. What she'd do, she told Joe, was to get pupils and get paid for teaching them—she'd still be working at her music while getting paid. The perfect solution! Joe felt a bit funny about his wife having to work to keep him and his career studies going, but he went along with it. Besides, even while he studied, he was painting, and who knows, he said, he might even be able to unload a painting on some poor unsuspecting buyer who was loaded with money.

Love knows about rules and always fulfills them, but it very often fulfills them by rising above them rather than confining itself to the letter.

For two or three days, Delia canvassed for pupils and came home one evening, bubbling with delight. "I've got a pupil...lovely family...a general...General A. B. Pinkey...his daughter...gorgeous house...Clementina... love her already. She's a delicate thing—always dresses in white...only eighteen...three lessons a week...five dollars a lesson! Isn't it wonderful? When I get a couple more pupils...back to Rosenstock..." Beside herself with pleasure she was.

Joe protested. She hung on his neck: "Don't be silly," she said; "fifteen dollars a week is more than enough." He mustn't think of leaving Mr. Magister. He reluctantly agreed, and they dived into their vegetables while Joe told her how pleased Magister was with the sketches he'd made in the park. He'd even gotten a couple hung in a local businessman's window. You never know, he might sell a few, and Delia could get back to her studies.

A week of skimpy and early breakfasts passed, 7:00 A.M. departures and 7:00 P.M. returns, but at the week's end, Delia, weary and triumphant, laid down three five-dollar bills. Why was she so weary? Well, sometimes Clementina wearied her. It was obvious that she didn't practice a lot, and she had to be reminded of things over and over again. But General Pinkey—a dear old man, a widower—would stand by the piano while his daughter played, tugging at his white goatee, asking about semiquavers and demi-semiquavers. Pinkey's brother was once Minister to Bolivia, what a dear child

Clementina was, and the décor of the house, well, *wonderful* wasn't the word for it.

Joe waited until she took a breath and then, with a flourish, laid out a ten, a five, a two, and a one—eighteen dollars. "Sold that water-color of the obelisk to a man from Peoria," he chuckled. Fat man with a woolen muffler and a quill toothpick; thought he was buying a painting of a windmill at first—in from "the sticks"—and what's more, he'd ordered an oil sketch of the freight depot. Thirty-three dollars—they were rich.

The next Saturday, Joe, with what seemed a lot of dark paint that needed washing off, was first home and laid out his eighteen dollars on the parlor table. Delia arrived a half-hour later, her right hand bandaged and fifteen dollars to flourish.

What happened? Clementina insisted on toast and melted cheese after the lesson. Can you imagine "Welsh Rabbit" at five in the afternoon? The girl tipped the hot dish over her hand…the general rushed down and got someone—the furnace man, they said—to get oil from the drugstore and stuff to wrap it up. Oh well, what's done is done. She saw the money and asked if he'd sold the other painting. Yep, the guy from Peoria was a sucker for his work and—"What time this afternoon did you burn your hand, Dele?" he asked casually. About five o'clock, she told him, and he should have seen General Pinkey's panic—

"Sit down here a moment, Dele," he said gently, putting his arm around her. "What have you been doing for the last two weeks?" he asked. She bluffed it out for a moment or two, with eyes full of love and stubbornness, but at last out came the truth along with some tears. She couldn't get any pupils, so she had taken a job ironing shirts at a laundry and a girl had set a hot iron on her hand. "You're not angry, are you, Joe?" Besides, she timidly reminded him, "If I hadn't got the work, you mightn't have sold your sketches to that man from Peoria."

"He wasn't from Peoria," Joe said slowly.

"Well, it doesn't matter where he was from. How clever you are, Joe— and—kiss me, Joe—and what made you ever suspect that I wasn't giving music lessons to Clementina?"

"I didn't," said Joe, "until tonight. And I wouldn't have then, only I sent up this cotton waste and oil from the engine room this afternoon for a girl upstairs who had her hand burned with a smoothing-iron. I've been firing the engine in that laundry for the last two weeks."

And they both laughed as they compared their artistic "sweet deceits" that hid their loving sacrifices.

The O. Henry story I've just rehearsed illustrates what the philosopher and ethicist T. E. Jessop meant when he said of love: "It is full of considerate lies and sweet deceits, of charming impetuosities and gracious whims and magnificent improprieties.… It has no…constitution drawn up with pedantic precision to define obligations and safeguard rights, to set forth just how much others should do for us and just how little we should do for others."

Love knows about rules and always fulfills them, but it very often fulfills them by rising above them rather than confining itself to the letter. The motivation that goes into the making of rules can become the very inspiration to do more than the rules can or do call for. This is part of the reason that love makes for an adventurous life and lovers need never be bored.

i love how you
gallantly
pretend

i love you

 [Love] is full of considerate lies and *sweet* deceits, of *charming* impetuosities and gracious whims and *magnificent* improprieties.

T. E. Jessop

I love thee with a love I seemed to lose
With my lost saints,—
I love thee with the breath,
Smiles, tears, of all my life!—
and, if God choose,
I shall but love thee better after death.

ELIZABETH BARRETT BROWNING

A DOZEN

i love you

for helping me see that life, not death, is forever

The girls obviously didn't think much of me when I was a teenager, so when this pretty girl called Ethel gave me more than a second look, I followed her like a lap dog and managed not to drive her away. Early in our relationship, we were walking down by the shoreline one evening, buttoned-up sweaters and scarves against the crisp air, arms around each other, her head in my chest, and she said to me, slowly but with some conviction, "Jim, I'm stuck on you." Forever unsure of myself, but with a nice warm flush rising in my face and wanting to hear more, I said: "Aw, you're probably just saying that." She said, "I'm not; my hair's caught in one of your buttons." You don't believe it, huh? Well...it's the kind of thing she might have said, for Ethel has a soft directness with her that I envy at times.

I could easily give you the impression that our relationship over forty-three years of marriage has been ideal—that's just not so; but it's been a great adventure for all that. It's a marriage that's blossomed into friendship or maybe friendship that's blossomed into marriage. Perhaps something of both.

I've made more than my share of mistakes over the years and have many things to regret—things I can hardly bear to think about, much less reflect on—but there are some incidents that make me smile with pleasure and contentment, memories I bring out and examine more than occasionally.

There was the time we were going through the Scriptures together and came across that enigmatic passage in Matthew 22:30 when Jesus' opponents asked him whose wife an often-married woman would be at the resurrection. Christ told them that husband-wife relationships wouldn't exist then. I said to Ethel, "That means you and I won't be husband and wife in that new phase of our existence." She struggled with that for a moment, not happy with it at all, but saying nothing. Seeing she was crestfallen and wanting to cheer her up, I quickly added, "But we'll know each other, we'll still be *us*, and we'll be friends forever."

That changed things totally, but it still moved her close to tears. She put her little hands over her eyes to hide behind them, and then, from between her fingers, her eyes glistening with tears, she looked out at me and said, "Is that really true, Jim?" By now I was all tenderness, moved by her pleasure and pleased at her joy, and I gently assured her it was. Friends forever.

This reminds me of William Cowper, who wrote some famous hymns, including *God Moves in a Mysterious Way*. He wrote to a cousin he adored and

The present joy and incredible potential that friendship has assures us there's more to life than what we can grasp in the here and now.

ended his letter with these words: "There is not room enough for friendship to unfold itself in full bloom in such a nook of life as this. Therefore I am, and must, and will be, Yours forever."

It's at this point I see clearly how important friends are one to another. The present joy and incredible potential that friendship has assures us there's more to life than what we can grasp in the here and now. God came in Christ to give us more than this. Life goes on and on and on. And because this is true, the face of death is transformed. *Of course* we hurt sorely when our beloved dies, but if the Christian faith is true, those who die in Christ are blessed—they're well! And while we weep for ourselves because we miss them so, we can rejoice for them because they're having "the time of their lives."

Think of the crowd of questions already answered for them while we stumble around in hopeful search. And how happy they must be for *us*, whom they've loved so long, knowing what's ahead for us when our time comes. They must be filled with joyful anticipation of our arrival, hardly able to wait to see our response to the profound breadth and depth of life—a profoundness we aren't able to grasp right now. Part of our beloveds' joy in that expanded phase of life must be their looking for the glorious moment when we win through to our place at their side. "See?" they'll say laughing, "You see how wonderful it is? And you were feeling a bit sorrowful for *me?* This life is filled with a host of answers and even more glorious mysteries. How thrilled I am that we're friends forever in a life like this."

And won't such people look at each other with new depth and appreciation? Won't they tell each other how glad they are that they helped one another to hunger for light, for better, and for more than even their lovely previous history together had already given them?

If all this is true and if death well prepared for is immeasurable gain, shouldn't that strengthen our resolve to help each other prepare? Shouldn't we view our friendships as the "forever" kind even now? And won't a gladder view of death have its good influence here and now? Won't the joy of our absent beloveds make it that bit easier to be without them for a while? And won't we be glad beyond words for all the warmth, the patience, the encouragement, the forgiveness, the joy and pleasure, the protection we gave and received in this the beginning phase of limitless life? Yes, we will; we will! Forever friends will feel that.

i love you
for helping me
see that life,
not death,
is forever

i love you

There is not room enough for *friendship* to unfold itself in *full bloom* in such a nook of life as this. Therefore I am, and must, and will be, *Yours forever*.

William Cowper

$\mathcal{L}$ove knows no limit to its endurance, no end to its trust, no fading of its hope; it can outlast anything. It is, in fact, the one thing that still stands when all else has fallen.

1 CORINTHIANS 13:7–8 PHILLIPS

NOTES

ONE. Don't Take the Girl

The opening quote is from the song "You and Me against the World," words and music by Paul Williams and Ken Ascher, Almo Music Corporation, Warner Chappell Music Inc. Used with permission.

From the song "Don't Take the Girl," words and music by Craig Martin and Larry W. Johnson, Eric Zanetis Publishing Co., Warner Chappell Music Inc. Used with permission.

From the song "If I Had My Life to Live Over," words and music by Harry Tobias, Moe Jaffe, and Larry Vincent, Warner Chappell Music Inc., 1939. Used with permission.

TWO. Ain't Love Grand

The opening quote is from Portia to Bassanio in Shakespeare's *Merchant of Venice*, act 3, scene 2. She's telling him that what he sees he gets but that she wishes she were more for his sake. Ain't it grand?

From the song "If I Had You," words and music by Ted Shapiro, Jimmy Campbell, and Reg Connelly, Campbell & Connelly Inc., 1929. Used with permission.

The C. J. Dennis poem/book is *The Songs of a Sentimental Bloke*, Selwyn & Blount, London, 1936, 42, 49, 112, 139–140.

THREE. A Midsummer's Knight

The opening quote is from the poem "True Love," quoted by Don E. Boatman, *Out of My Treasure*, College Press, Joplin, Mo., 1965, 192.

The story of Gaines is from the book *More O. Henry*, Hodder & Stoughton, London, 1959, introduced by James Hilton, from the story "A Misdummer Knight's Dream."

The Gilbert Murray quote can be found in H. E. Fosdick's *Meaning of Service*, Abingdon Press, Nashville, 1983, 198.

From the song "That's Enough for Me," words and music by Paul Williams, Irving Music Inc. Used with permission.

FOUR. Don't Shilly-Shally

The opening quote from F. W. Robertson is found in *Sermons*, 4th Series, Kegan, Paul, Trench & Co., London, 1885, 131.

From the song "What Will My Mary Say," words and music by P. Vance and E. Snyder, Music Sales Corporation, 1986. Used with permission.

The Croft poem is from *The Best Loved Poems of the American People*, Doubleday & Company Inc., New York, 1936, 25.

FIVE. What Would My Ethel Say?

The opening quote is from "In Memoriam." *The Cambridge History of English and American Literature*, XIII, Cambridge, England, 1907–1921.

The Arthur Gossip incident is rehearsed in his *In Christ's Stead*, Hodder & Stoughton, London, 1925, 79–80.

SIX. Mrs. Micawber and I

The opening quote is from *The Little Prince*, Harcourt, Brace & World Inc., New York, 1971.

The A. J. Gordon story is from his *A Touch of Wonder*, Fleming H. Revell, Old Tappan, N.J., 1982. Used with permission.

From the song "You Needed Me," words and music by Charles R. Goodman, Warner Chappell Music Inc. Used with permission.

SEVEN. "My Dearest Vera"

The opening quote is from Dale Wasserman's stage play based on Cervantes' *Don Quixote* and shown in the movie *The Man of La Mancha*, 1972, directed by Athur Hiller, with a Joe Darian & Mitch Leigh score. The critics regard the movie as a complete disaster. I loved it.

Allain's story is from Richard Selzer's *Rituals of Surgery*, Simon and Schuster Inc., New York, 1974. Used with permission. Reprinted with permission from the April 1981 *Reader's Digest*.

The *Forever Darling* quotation is from the movie directed by Andrew Hall, starring James Mason, Lucille Ball, and Desi Arnez. A tolerable movie, but no classic.

EIGHT. Ethel, Loss, and Ethel Again

The Huxley quotations are from *A Brave New World*, Harper Collins, New York, 1972. Used with permission.

Browning's poem is found in many anthologies of his work.

NINE. You and Me against the World

The opening quote is from "Rabbi Ben Ezra." *Browning: A Selection by W. E. Williams*, Penguin Books, Middlesex, England, 1984, 258.

From the song "You and Me against the World," words and music by Paul Williams and Ken Ascher, Almo Music Corporation. Used with permission.

The Banks quotation is from *Hero Tales from Sacred Story*, Funk & Wagnalls, New York, 1897, 255.

TEN. Tamed

The Little Prince, Antoine de Saint-Exupéry, Harcourt, Brace & World Inc., New York, 1971.

ELEVEN. Welsh Rabbit in the Afternoon

The opening quote is from Kipling's famous poem "If." *The Works of Rudyard Kipling,* The Wordsworth Poetry Library, Hertfordshire, England, 1994.

The story of Joe and Delia is from "A Service of Love," found in *The Best of O. Henry,* Hodder & Stoughton, London, 1952.

The T. E. Jessop quote is from his *Law and Love*, SCM Press, London, 1940, 185.

A DOZEN. Friends Forever

The opening quotation is a piece from her famous poem *How Do I Love Thee?* addressed to her husband, Robert Browning.